ISBN: 979-8-9919096-0-0

Marly Camino
www.marlycamino.com
Contact at info@marlycamino.com

The Self Academy & Club
www.theself.club
Contact at hello@theself.club

It is not what you
acquire or where you
get to, but rather
who you become.

Table of Contents

Welcome Home

Life reflects the Camino, and the Camino reflects life.

We are all on a soul journey; a path filled with experiences, successes and failures, hopes and fears, joy and pain, connection and disconnection. **To be human** is to embrace all the dualities and paradoxes of this physical existence.

Although in this material world it is easy to fall under the illusion that what we are looking for is somewhere, or something, or someone – true wisdom whispers to us that the answers are within. It's time to listen to those whispers.

On this journey, it is not where you get to, but rather who you become. You are here to feel, to discover your truest essence, be Loved and to Love. With a capital L.

I invite you to go beyond the expectations and instructions of society **in search for your deepest Self.** There is a wisdom that emerges when you let life in, when you surrender to its flow and allow it to move you. This path of honesty and vulnerability isn't always easy for the ego, but finding the courage to face this discomfort is where true spiritual transformation begins.

I wrote these reflections for our Pilgrims with so much Love, and have now turned them into this book due to popular demand! I hope these reflections become **a reminder and anchor** to the deeper part of you, guiding you on your journey home to yourself.

Big Love and Buen Camino.

Sami

Pilgrimage

"The real voyage of discovery consists not in seeking new landscapes, but in having new eyes."

Marcel Proust

Pilgrimage

There is a difference between traveling and going on a pilgrimage. When you travel, the external world is the protagonist. You go to see places and monuments and you use airplanes, trains, buses, and cars.

When you are a Pilgrim, you might still do some of those things, but the difference is that **you are protagonist and your body is your main vehicle**.

A pilgrimage is a **spiritual initiation**, every single time. It is a journey not only of the body but of the soul. When your soul decides to go on a pilgrimage, there is purpose. It is a journey of *self-reflection, self-discovery, and spiritual search* with experiences and messages for you every step. The question is, are you listening?

Pilgrim, open your eyes, open your mind, open your heart. The messages and shifts can be subtle or obvious, small or big. It is your job now to **attune to a new rhythm –** the rhythm of the Camino, of nature, and of life itself.

Everything on this pilgrimage is happening for you. *Don't be fooled.* The destination might seem to be a place on the map but it is truly a **treasure within yourself.**

Surrender to the becoming and welcome who you might become.

Pilgrimage

Reflect and write:

- What part of me brought me here?

- How is this special or different for me compared to other travels or journeys I have done in the past?

- What is my intention for this pilgrimage?

Invitation:

As your pilgrimage begins, start to **shift your mindset**. Start to become more present to everything around you. Reflect on one activity, thought, or 'distraction' you can give up for the duration of your pilgrimage.

Attitude

"Everything can be taken from a man
but one thing: the last of the human
freedoms – to choose one's attitude in
any given set of circumstances."

Viktor E. Frankl

Attitude

There aren't many things in our control. Attitude is one of the few that are. Pilgrim, it is now time to become more aware of the attitudes you have, and if they are serving you.

Your attitude taints your entire experience. If your attitude is negative, it is likely your experience will be too. Changing our attitude is always possible, but we become entrenched in old ways and forget this.

Our beliefs and expectations shape our entire life. When you understand this, you realize the power of choosing an attitude that is focused on gratitude and growth.

Empowering attitudes increase our mental and physical well-being. The Camino reminds you that **life is happening *for* you.** That nothing is a coincidence.

This way of thinking shifts your attitude from a victim mentality into **an empowered creator of your experience** and of your life where new realities are possible and available to you.

Pilgrim, don't let your attitude limit you, but rather, empower you. **Gratitude is always the best attitude.** Take yourself there as often as possible, going through all the ups and downs if often takes to get there again.

Attitude

Reflect and write:

- Are there any limiting beliefs or painful emotions tainting my attitude?

- How can I shift my attitude to create an even better experience for myself and those around me?

- What am I grateful for today? How does my attitude shift when I remember and focus on this?

Invitation:

Today, consciously **embrace an empowering or positive attitude or mindset** for your day. Perhaps a quote or affirmation could inspire you. Notice what it's like to embody this throughout your day.

The Unexpected

"If you want to make God laugh, tell
him about your plans."

Woody Allen

The Unexpected

There is a natural and beautiful side to expectations that comes from our **hopes, desires, and beliefs** that things could turn out a certain way. The optimist expects the best.

The shadow side is the part that come from our need for control, our perfectionism and our inner critic which create **pressure, demands, or perpetual disappointment**. Disappointment is when reality doesn't meet our expectations.

Expectations that are too high or unrealistic can lead to frustration, bitterness, and depression. The Camino often invites us to **reevaluate our expectations** about ourselves, about others, and about life.

Find the balance between allowing standards and hopes to motivate you while remaining open to the unexpected, unforeseeable turns & surprises life inevitably brings, that you will undoubtedly be able to handle.

Trust yourself and others to handle disappointment. When reality doesn't match our expectations, **trust that life has something even better in store**.

With an attitude of **gratitude, growth, and faith**, that is always the case. Release expectations and trust the unfolding of your Camino and of your life.

The Unexpected

Reflect and write:

- In which areas am I often disappointed or scared to disappoint others?

- What are my expectations and where do they stem from? Are they reasonable? Are they helpful?

- Are there any that I might want to let go of to feel lighter and free?

Invitation:

Today, practice **releasing all expectations**. Expect nothing and be surprised and accepting of everything. Imagine everything that happens is a gift from the universe. Notice how it feels inside of you to move through your day like this.

Acceptance & Surrender

"Accept – then act. Whatever the present moment contains, accept it as if you had chosen it. Always work with it, not against it.

Make it your friend and ally, not your enemy. This will miraculously transform your whole life."

Eckhart Tolle

Acceptance & Surrender

Acceptance is a state of **recognizing and embracing reality as it is,** without attempting to change or resist it. This process involves letting go- setting aside our stubborn ego, our mighty willpower, and our fervent hopes and expectations.

It is about being present with the reality of 'now' and not the what could or should be. Acceptance **requires the courage** to drop the often comforting illusions and fantasies of denial and come face to face with truth itself.

Acceptance is an active choice to surrender. It is not about giving up, but rather surrendering your ego and having an attitude of cooperation with the divine unfolding of life. It requires **trust, letting go,** and is an **act of faith.**

Acceptance creates a state of relaxation within your own self, where you are no longer fighting , resisting or controlling reality, but rather flowing with it.

Playing 'God' is a fantasy that gives us the illusion of control until we realize we are equally as fragile and ephemeral as we are strong and eternal. **Focus on what you can control**, and accept and let go of what you cannot.

Who would be crazy enough to try to fight a wave? **Pilgrim, learn to swim, dive or surf with the current, so you can finally be free.** Let God be God, you just have to be you.

Acceptance & Surrender

Reflect and write:

- What part of life or myself do I still resist? What is challenging for me to accept?

- Where is there tension in my body?

- What internal battle with reality would bring relief if I surrendered?

Invitation:

Take a deep breath now. Today, **practice radical acceptance.** Absolutely everything that happens, convenient or not, see it as the most perfect unfolding of reality designed by divinity.

Notice how it feels for your ego as you let go of control and trust the divine.

Past, **Present**, Future

"The only way to live is by accepting each minute as an unrepeatable miracle."

Tara Brach

Past, Present, Future

The past is gone. We can't change what happened, but by shifting how we relate to the past we can be free from it so that we can actually come fully into the present.

The future is a potential. You cannot control it, but only imagine it, wonder or worry about it, or shape it with the choices you make in the present.

The past and future don't really exist, except as constructs in our own minds. If you're constantly focusing on the past or the future, you're missing out on your life.

Life only happens in the now. Now is when you can smell the flowers, feel the wind or sun on your skin, taste delicious food, and get to know someone better. Now is when you have agency to act and affect change. Now is where all of your power lies. All of life is simply a series of 'nows'.

The Camino invites you to stop escaping and to be present every step. Drop your mind, drop your expectations, drop your control mechanisms, drop your phone while you're at it, and **choose to live this precious life** by being here now.

Use your six senses to take life in, connect with yourself, with others and with life as if every moment was a unique, unrepeatable moment, because they each are. Pilgrim, **the present moment is all you ever have. Don't miss it.**

Past, Present, Future

Reflect and write:

- Do I live more in the past, future, or the present?

- What do I avoid by escaping? Consider things within your own self like feelings, emotions, or external things.

- Today, how can I drop deeper into the present moment?

Invitation:

The breath anchors us to the present. Today, become **mindful of your breathing** and use it as an anchor to come back into the present moment.

Practice taking 3 deep belly breaths in different moments of the day, and notice how your awareness is pulled back into the present moment. Let go of the past and future as you breathe out.

Letting Go

"Some of us think holding on makes us
strong, but sometimes it is letting go."

Hermann Hesse

Letting Go

Our backpacks on the Camino reflect the metaphorical backpack we carry through life. Every item, even though it may seem small, carries a weight that we feel. Just as we carry physical items, we also bear emotional and mental burdens.

Over many kilometers, over many days, over many steps on our journey, this **weight can feel heavier and heavier**. Sometimes it is unbearable. Once it is too heavy to handle, **your body may protest**. It may whisper or scream, begging you to let go of some of the weight. Or your body may adapt, developing calluses, muscle or simply getting used to the chronic pain.

Sometimes our identity can get wrapped up with the pain and suffering, as if it were a part of us. However, you must remember that you **have the choice to let go.** You have the option to stop carrying whatever you are carrying, physically, emotionally or mentally, if you simply choose to. **Behind everything we can't let go, there is a pain we are unwilling to face.**

Pilgrim, have the courage to listen to what your body, heart, and soul are telling you so you don't prolong your suffering any longer. Free yourself from limiting constructs that only exist in your mind. **Pain is not your natural state, Love is.**

Letting Go

Reflect and write:

- What in my metaphorical backpack is heavy? What have I been carrying for too many kilometers or years? (Consider painful emotions like fears, grief, or anger).

- What do I fear might happen if I let go? What new, amazing possibility might open up if I let go?

Invitation:

After journaling today, **choose something you want to let go of.** Put the intention of this thing into an object and do something symbolic like give something away, burn it, or throw a stone into a river.

You may write something on a paper and burn it, or carry a stone representing that thing and throw into a river when you are ready. The object you choose is not as important as the intention you put behind it and your true willingness to let go.

When you let go of it, with curiosity start to explore who you are without this weight. Feel lighter and lighter, freer and freer.

Duality & Paradox

"Owning our story can be hard, but not nearly as difficult as spending our lives running from it. Embracing our vulnerabilities is risky but not nearly as dangerous as giving up on love and belonging and joy."

Brené Brown

Duality and Paradox

Contrast is what allows us to experience and embrace the wholeness of life. By knowing sadness, we know joy. Noise allows us to **enjoy the silence**. Being too selfless reminds us of the need to care for oneself. Our wounds reveal our gifts.

Freedom helps you value connection. Chaos helps us appreciate order. The feminine helps us understand the masculine. And visa versa. Sometimes the worst thing that ever happens to you turns out to be the best thing that ever happened to you.

Opposites are inevitably intertwined, defining each other and give meaning to the whole. Their tension and interplay opens us up to a more nuanced reality. Fear helps us discover courage, and we discover our true strength through vulnerability. **Duality is not about separation, but about the unity within contrast.**

Do not box life, yourself, or others into a one-sided box or perspective. Release your judgments and opinions so and ask yourself what else is possible. Contrast is what gives you the full picture.

Allow yourself to explore and experience contrast so that you may know who you truly are. Our soul came here to express itself fully, to embrace wholeness. Only in the darkness can you see the stars.

Duality and Paradox

Reflect and write:

- Has anything shocked me so far?

- Where do I still hold rigid judgments or one-sided perspectives?

- What would the opposite of strong perspective I hold? In what ways could that reality also be true?

Invitation:

Practice doing the **opposite of something you normally do** today. This could be an action or a thought. Perhaps if you're usually speak a lot, today you can be quiet. Or if you defend something often, you can try and take the opposite stance as an exercise in expanding the mind to hold multiple truths.

Notice who you are and how you feel about yourself in that contrasting reality.

Ego & Humility

The ego is only an illusion, but a very influential one. Letting the ego-illusion become your identity can prevent you from knowing your true self.

Wayne Dyer

Ego and Humility

The ego is the part of ourselves that protects, defends, and helps us to survive. It is the ego that always wants more money, more power, more things, more control. **This survival mode is a primal state and is where all fear stems from.**

Living in a fear state keeps us stuck and our nervous system on alert, seeing the world as a threat we must defend ourselves from. From this place of lack, the pursuit is endless and futile because **nothing is ever enough.**

In its pursuit of self-preservation, it separate us from our authentic selves and authentic connection with others. It is only through knowing our true selves that we can let go of the exhausting need for external validation, approval, recognition, and admiration from others.

The spiritual path asks us to transcend the ego and to go beyond fear and control to something bigger. The Camino asks us for the **humility to drop the ego's false masks, defense mechanisms, and grandiose self-image** to connect with something bigger than ourselves.

There is nothing to prove. There is nothing to defend. When there is less ego there is more room for God.

You are important, you are enough, you are worthy, you are loved. **You are necessary.** You are a child of this universe. When you truly remember this, you come back into your heart and into the infinite Love that you are.

Ego and Humility

Reflect and write:

- What experiences have humbled me in the past?

- How does my ego show up in moments of conflict or challenge? What does it seek to protect?

- Who do I compare yourself to most, and what does this say about my ego's desires or insecurities?

Invitation:

Today, practice **noticing the way your ego shows up** throughout your day. Notice if you're trying to prove anything to anyone or yourself. Notice if you're trying to control an outcome. Notice the role of the ego and what it is trying to protect.

Acknowledge it, thank it, and let your soul, or God, have the steering wheel instead. Notice how that feels.

Diversity

"Our ability to reach unity in
diversity will be the beauty and the
test of our civilization."

Mahatma Gandhi

Diversity

If there is one thing that characterizes the humanity, it is diversity. Our lives can often become comfort zones of safe, known, homogenous behaviors, ways of thinking, people, and ideas.

The Camino is a melting pot of humanity. It doesn't matter where you come from, what you do, why you are here – we are now pilgrims on the Camino de Santiago. Walking with purpose and intention, being both humbled and marveled by our own bodies reminds us of our humanity, of our souls, of the ultimate life journey we are all on.

By opening ourselves up to different perspectives, **we learn to listen with curiosity and respect.** This practice deepens our understanding of others' struggles, joys, and challenges.

Recognize that everyone brings something unique to the table. There is something original and noteworthy about everyone's experience of reality, all equally as valid.

You say 'Buen Camino' to everyone on your path, because everyone, no matter the background, color, religion, history, gender or race, **everyone deserves to have a Buen Camino.**

Everyone deserves respect and Love. Bumping against with diversity is your opportunity to embrace your humanity and develop your empathy. We are all part of the fabric of the universe, get to know the fellow creatures on this journey, because **we are all in this together.**

Diversity

Reflect and write:

- Reflect on the diverse encounters I have had so far on the Camino. How have these interactions enriched my journey?

- Who have I met that comes from a vastly different background than mine. What did this interaction teach me about life, humanity, or myself?

Invitation:

Reflect on **who or what you judge or reject**. Perhaps it is a type of person, or a behavior. Today, open your mind towards it.

Send love and acceptance towards that too. Make space for it in your heart. You don't have to understand it, you just have to respect it and allow it to be.

Vulnerability

"A tolerance of weakness is a prerequisite for the discovery of power, for any exercise of strength motivated by an avoidance of weakness is not genuine power."

Thomas Moore

Vulnerability

To be human is to be vulnerable. Being alive in itself is a vulnerable thing. We have basic needs and we depend on others for our survival since we are babies until the day we die. We need food, water, air, physical touch, affection, belonging and much more. These human needs make us vulnerable. That is the truth and it is so beautiful. Moreover, most aspects of life itself are **completely out of our control.**

Our society often values strength and independence which often makes us want to hide our inherent vulnerability, pretend we're strong, hide our true feelings, deny our own needs, and to pretend we're in control when it's really anxiety.

The truth can often inevitably be a vulnerable thing. And that is why vulnerability is liberating, because the truth will always set you free. **It takes immense courage to be open**, to show our authentic selves, and to acknowledge and share our fears, uncertainties, and flaws instead of showing our mask.

When we aim to be real instead of perfect, we open the true gateway to connection. When we recognize we're not perfect and will never be, we surrender our humble hearts and become more accepting of all of life.

Pilgrim, stop pretending and show yourself. You can't hide from God. Choosing to be vulnerable and show yourself as you truly are, despite consequences, is **the bravest thing a human being can ever do.** Show your truth and have faith, that is exactly what the universe needs – the real you.

Vulnerability

Reflect and write:

- What aspects of myself or my life am I ashamed of? What would I prefer people didn't know about me?

- What can I be more honest with myself about? What about with others?

- Is there something I have been wanting to explore but have been scared or simply haven't had the time for?

Invitation:

Today, find an appropriate time to **share something** that is vulnerable for you. It could be something that is difficult, painful, or that you have shame around.

You can share it with a perfect stranger, or with someone you know. Notice how vulnerability feels for you in your body.

Interdependence

"We're all just walking each
other home."

Ram Dass

Interdependence

We need other people, not only to survive, but to experience joy, fulfillment, and love. It is vulnerable to need anything and especially to need others and these needs are also **what makes us human**. Feeling alone and like everything depends on you is a heavy burden to carry.

You are strong, yes. You are capable, yes. *And* you are allowed to rely on others. You need to be able to rely on others.

The sweet spot between dependence and independence is **interdependence**. No being can exist or function in isolation. Everything is influenced by and has an impact on other things or beings.

Nature is the ultimate example of interdependence. Every living organism, from the smallest insect to the largest animal, plays a crucial role in the ecosystem.

We as humans are part of a beautiful ecosystem working together to maintain balance and harmony. **More is possible when we work together.** The Camino invites us to ask for help and to lend a helping hand, to both give and receive.

Being of service to others fosters community, co-creation, and Love. And remember that allowing ourselves to receive gives others the gift of giving.

Interdependence

Reflect and write:

- How do my actions or mere presence impact those in my life? Who impacts me the most and how?

- Is it easier for me to give or receive? How do each feel for me?

- What could I ask for help with that would make my life so much easier, instead of having to carry the burden alone?

Invitation:

Today, **ask for help** with something you can do on your own *and* **lend a helping hand** with something just for the sake of helping and being of service. Notice how giving and receiving feel for you.

Power

"Our deepest fear is not that we are
inadequate. Our deepest fear is that we
are powerful beyond measure."

Marianne Williamson

Power

Pilgrim, **you are far more powerful than you realize.** Your power lies not in controlling everything around you, but in the way you choose to show up for yourself and for life.

The realization that you are a sovereign, powerful human being is one that many fear. Because, indeed, with great power comes great responsibility. It takes courage to step into this truth. Many avoid it, preferring to stay small or comfortable, relinquishing their power to fears, doubts, or the opinions of others. Not you, though. You chose courage.

True power isn't about force – it's about presence. It's the quiet strength of standing in your truth, of knowing that no matter what happens, you have the ability to respond with courage, clarity, and love.

Being in your power is different from having power over someone. Any attempt to demonstrate power comes from a place of fear – fear of losing it. The one who truly knows their power has nothing to prove, nothing to force. True power does not grip; it flows. True power does not fear; it trusts.

The Camino reminds us that power doesn't come from the outside – it's built from within. It's the strength to take one more step when you're tired. It's the wisdom to pause when you need rest. It's the faith to trust the path, even when it's unclear.

Many religions teach, or hint, that the divine resides within us. How do we reconcile the paradox that God is both something we surrender to and something within us? This is one of the most profound mysteries of being human. Your power is not separate from the divine, it is a reflection of it. **Embrace it.**

Power

Reflect and write:

- What do I complain about often?

- Is there anything or anyone I blame?

- What would a narrative shift into my power look like in these areas? What are my lessons in these areas, knowing I have the power to do/change anything?

Invitation:

Today, look into the mirror and affirm **"I am powerful."** Notice how it feels and what it brings up for you. You can repeat it a few times.

Simultaneously, practice seeing every human being you come across as profoundly powerful and intelligent. Notice the shift when you see yourself and others as powerful changes?

Purpose

"The purpose of life is not to be happy. It is to be useful, to be honorable, to be compassionate, to have it make some difference that you have lived and lived well."

Ralph Waldo Emerson

Purpose

To have a sense of purpose is to have an internal, renewable engine that fuels your entire existence. Purpose is not static, it will transform throughout your life. You will be confused about it at times, you will refine it, you will transform it and mostly, it will transform you if you give yourself to it.

There are aspects in our life that unfailingly point towards your purpose. Your **natural strengths and skills** is one of them. It is part of your purpose to gift them to humanity.

Another aspect that points towards your purpose is **your values and passions**. What your heart truly cares for, the things that motivate you and animate your emotions are one of the ways in which your purpose speaks to you.

What you have been through in this life is also part of your purpose. **The joy and the pain you have experienced are gifts from life that you can share with others** for our collective evolution. Remember that pain comes to teach you, never to punish you.

Put yourself at the service of this world. Purpose is not a destination, **it is a never-ending fuel** that you discover when you realize how much the world needs you.

Pilgrim, nothing about you is a coincidence. You are not by chance. **You were created on purpose and with a purpose.** Find it and give it away. Humanity needs you.

Purpose

Reflect and write:

- When do I feel the most alive, aligned, and on purpose? How can I do more of that in my life?

- What or who drains my energy and life force? Can I reduce the presence of this in your life? Reflect on the reason it is still there (guilt, obligation, fear, etc.)

- What significant personal experience has changed you?

Invitation:

Today, **reflect on your purpose.** Reflect on what has fueled you throughout your life. Find a moment to share a significant personal experience with others – one that has changed you somehow. Notice the effect it has when you do it.

Soul

"The desire to know your own soul
will end all other desires."

Rumi

Soul

Your soul is the eternal, divine part of you, beyond the physical body. It is not for me, or anyone, to tell you what the soul is, but rather to invite you to explore this powerful part of yourself on your own.

Attuning to the **language of the soul** requires new abilities and a new disposition. This language is subtle and nuanced, it's not necessarily rational, nor linear.

To speak 'soul', you must **open yourself up to mystery** and to the unknown, which our ego often avoids out of fear and loss of control. The soul knows no time, it only knows Love. Through the **gateway of your heart** you can start to access the secret wisdom of your soul.

Synchronicities and so-called 'coincidences' are often 'Godscideneces' – events that are trying to give us subtle signs. Connecting with your soul will shatter your mental maps of reality and open you to the truth of what is beyond.

When we start to know the soul, we start to **let go of the idea that death is something to be feared.** The soul never dies because energy cannot die, it can only ever be transformed. What we call 'death' is the soul coming back to where it came from, simply going back home.

Pilgrim, this body is a temporary loan. Enjoy life, but don't become attached to it. Enjoy the consciousness available to you by being human. Dance, laugh, read poetry, hug a tree, talk to a bird, look at the clouds. Get out of your mind and into the magic of your soul. It has been waiting for you.

Soul

Reflect and write:

- What is my relationship to my soul? How do I think it tries to speak to me? (Think about my intuition)

- What would it look like for me to cultivate a relationship with my soul? What activities would that entail for me?

Invitation:

Place your hands over your heart and breathe in. Today, **live from your soul.** Practice getting out of your mind and ask your heart and soul what they desire. It doesn't matter if it feels silly, try it.

In fact, do something silly that you genuinely enjoy, especially if they seem like a 'waste of time'. Take time for something you usually don't make time for. Notice how it feels to show up from this part of you.

Together
We Walk.

Just like you are on your own personal journey in this lifetime, so is every other human being, and **so is all of humanity.** There is a collective journey we are all a part of.

Each generation of humans has a responsibility to take us beyond our own ego, into **a new vision for humanity anchored in Love.**

And each individual, starting with you, has the capacity to be a significant part of that. **Your inner work has a ripple effect on the entire universe.**

Thank you for your courage pilgrim.

Buen Camino, always.

Samantha

About **Samantha**

Samantha Sacchi Muci is the **co-founder of Marly Camino,** a family business she lovingly created with her mother, Ligia Muci Ramos, affectionately known as Marly. Since 2009, they've had the privilege of guiding thousands of pilgrims from all over the world along the magical Camino de Santiago, sharing in the deeply transformative power of the journey.

Born in Venezuela and raised between the U.S. And Spain, Samantha's life has been a mosaic of experiences across continents, immersed in diverse cultures and languages. This rich **global perspective**, combined with her deeply reflective soul, is at the heart of her work and teachings. She walks alongside others, creating spaces where people can reconnect with their own inner wisdom.

A consultant, coach, teacher, and facilitator, Samantha's work centers on inner growth and the need to **transform how we learn, live, and lead.**

She **founded The Self Academy & Club,** a community dedicated to offering transformative programs and experiences for individuals and purpose-driven organizations. Whether collaborating with universities in Australia, organizations in the Middle East, or individuals, her mission is the same: to remind people of **what it truly means to be human.**

Samantha's passion for healing and self-discovery stems from her own life. As a young girl and adult, she struggled deeply with **self-doubt and insecurity**, battles that left her questioning her worth.

Through **her own journey of healing and self-love**, she found not only her strength but also a profound empathy for others – especially women – who face similar internal struggles.

This personal experience fuels her desire to empower others, offering tools for self-awareness, emotional-spiritual intelligence, and resilience.

At the heart of her work lies a **vision of a more conscious and compassionate world.** Samantha believes that by embracing our humanity – our strengths, vulnerabilities, and everything in between – we can create a society that honors connection, self-responsibility, and collective well-being.

Through her teaching, writing, and facilitation, Samantha invites people to step into their own power and become creators of **meaningful, soul-aligned lives.** She considers herself a pilgrim of life too – always learning, growing, and discovering, one step at a time.

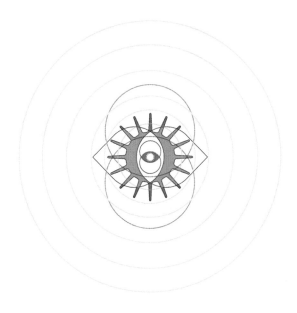

About **Marly**

"The Camino truly marked me, helping me overcome difficult moments and make some of the most important decisions in my life.

Now, it brings me immense joy—not only walking it myself but offering it to so many others. Witnessing their journeys and hearing their experiences has only deepened my belief that the Camino is a true gift from Life.

For me, walking the Camino is always a positive experience, and its effects don't end when I arrive in Santiago. The lessons I've learned stay with me, becoming **an integral part of who I am.**

I've come to understand that my inner strength, desire, and will are far more important than physical preparation. What matters most is the confidence I've gained in myself. This transformation has changed my life, and it's my greatest joy to help others experience their own inner journey.

At Marly Camino, we dedicate ourselves to the Camino de Santiago because we want to share the profound gifts it offers—a **lifelong connection to joy, growth, and transformation.**

Our goal has always been to make the Camino as life-changing for others as it has been for me. If we are open and willing, the Camino has the power to inspire changes that go far beyond the journey itself."

"Have wings that feared
ever touched the sun?

I was born when all
I once feared -
**I could
love.**"

-Rabia Al Basri

Made in the USA
Las Vegas, NV
15 December 2024

14442147R00031